51 Ways to Xpress
Love to Yourself

Written By: Jarell Rochelle
Edited By: Jarell and Madeline
Rochelle

Table of Contents

Preface

It's 2016, and I just married my beautiful wife on an Easter Sunday that took place in March (which won't happen again until 2035!). Talk about a miracle of sweet baby Jesus! On top of that, the venue was never supposed to be booked on Easter, and we were the first and only wedding to have had that privilege! It was just a magnificent day overall, and the favor leading up to it was supernatural. The wedding ceremony was beautiful. My bride looked like a girl on the cover of a 40s magazine. Classically beautiful! Our theme was "All blue everything," so naturally everyone wore blue, the cakes were blue, the decorations were blue, we even had an all-blue candy bar! We set up an art gallery with everyone's picture who came to the wedding and created art pieces that people had the chance to view for their personal satisfaction. If I do say so myself, it was one of the most creative, low-budget, amazing weddings that has ever taken place. There was so much JOY in the room! Even my dance crew was there! We partied, shared words, and danced all night long! So many different people from different cultures came together to honor me and my wife. I didn't know that we were ushering in what felt like a new wave of an otherwise bright season, and oh how magnificent this season would be!

This would sound like a set up for a perfect story; but then, God spoke a word…

Have you ever gotten a word, and you knew it was what God wanted you to do; BUT you did not want to do it? Yep, that was me for all of 2016. After all this goodness, life, and fun, God said firmly, yet in a still, soft voice, "I need you to leave your comfort in every way because I am about to deconstruct your life, building you and your family from the ground up, IN Me. I am about to build a NEW person that no one has ever seen… not even you; LEAVE your home, leave your family, leave your "friends," because I have something for you to do. Oh, and I am not going to give you all the details, but just walk in faith…" When I heard that, I was unsure and often asked the question, "Yeah, but why?" I kept asking, but the more I asked, the more I knew the answer didn't matter as much as my response to this word. "But, Father,' I said. "It feels so comfortable here, it feels so effortless, it feels like I don't even have to try…" All my reasons bucking back happened to be the same reasons why I had to leave (hindsight), but my unhealthy self-image kept me from seeing it. I was growing too complacent and underwhelmingly average, lost in the crowd, never really standing out. Let me tell anyone who is reading, you were meant for so much more than average, you were meant for greatness, to cover expansive territory, but you have to love yourself in order to see your greatest potential. I couldn't see it, I was blinded, BUT my spirit knew better; it was time to move on. Flash forward though two and a half years after the wedding. I was a prominent professional dancer in the local Houston dance scene, which God asked me to give up without an explanation. I was asked to relinquish friendships of years, with people I thought I would spend the rest of my life with because of the bonds we shared. I was asked to move away from Houston with my wife into the small town of Huntsville, Texas with no freestyle dance community at all. While living in Huntsville, I went back to compete in Houston for an event and ended up getting injured and could no longer do the one thing that gave me joy (which was dancing for seven months straight). After this injury, I opened my home to a brother who was incarcerated (for two years), whom my wife, my mom, and I supported financially and emotionally while in prison. He was released and came to live with us in our home, with my newborn child; then, in the worse kind of way, he turned his back on me with false accusations of my character. I had to lose him as well.

I had to intentionally distance myself from family members because, while I loved them, my life had become so broken, the only one I needed to hear from was God and anything that was not Him or was a distraction from hearing Him I had to cut loose. And, to add to the chaos, I had to figure out a new marriage, of which I had no experience in, while introducing my daughter into my world of chaos; understanding how to be a father, who couldn't find work and was depending on God's grace and my wife to help us in a season where I was so depressed that I became debilitated, unable to help myself. Sounds like fun time, right?

No, it sounds like a life of raw faith, and this book is for anyone who asks the questions, "Am I the only one with a jacked-up life? Trying to figure it out?" No, you are not. Not even close.

As stated above, this book was written because I was ALONE for two years with myself and in extreme doubt of the future because of the mistakes I made in the past. Before this point, it was easy to walk in faith, I had the support of the church, I had many friends keeping me busy with distractions, and I had work. I thought I was at the height of my faith, but I had only begun to understand the truth of the five-letter word. Faith is not faith without opposition and trial. I soon learned that REAL faith can only be illuminated when the light within you shines BRIGHTER than the darkness surrounding you. God stripped me of every false pretense that I thought held me up and showed me who I really was. When I was alone and silent, the greatest revelation came to me and was the inspiration for this book. The reason I had to give up those things was because they were a reflection of the false love I had accepted for myself and were not the truest reality of who I was created to be. A wise man once said, "We accept the love we believe we deserve." And because I had developed a savior complex, I believed that I was obligated to help anyone who came toward me. I even found purpose in making other people's lives better, while disregarding my own. This revelation was life changing. This experience forced me to go beyond the guards I put up and allowed me to see who I really was. I looked in the mirror and for some time struggled to look this foreign man in the eyes. I had never fully examined him, because I never took the time to LOVE myself. The time spent in exile away from every distraction brought me to a place where I could no longer hide from myself. I was forced to take the mask off, be broken, yet proudly say, "I am still worth it." Only later did I realize that this message of pain would soon be a turning point of my life's ministry, if I could just stick it out long enough and fight the battle in front of me. Without medicating it, without avoiding it, without placing the blame on someone else. I had to meet myself and love all of me.

This book is for the people who keep themselves distracted with busy works but don't really want to sit at the feet of Jesus the way Mary did. This book is for those who had everyone walk out on them and are hopeless in their thought that things will not turn around. This is for the little Shepard boy, like David working in the field, wondering when their time is going to come. This book was written by a man who asked himself, *Do I know how to love myself, and is it possible that God can love me and use me in the process?*

Have hope, there is beauty in the pain, and the only way go is through it.

So, why is loving myself so important? Seems a bit egotistical, doesn't it? No, not at all. In fact, it is quite the opposite, and a Kingdom Value. In Mark 12:30-31 It says the GREATEST commandments is *"Love the Lord your God with all your heart and all you soul and with all your mind and your strength."* The church does a pretty good job facilitating/teaching that type of love for God. So, as a body of believers, I believe that everyone has a pretty good understanding of what it means to love God (obedience to Him and His words), but something that is often overlooked is HOW to love ourselves. There aren't too many points in the Bible or spiritual books where it speaks in depth about self-love and HOW to produce it in a healthy way. The media often pushes loving other people more than yourself, as if it is some noble and righteous act; and while this ideology is a nice sentiment, I do not think God is saying to love other people and forget yourself. In fact, the scripture tells an entirely different story, it says (paraphrased) *"your capacity to love others is based on the true love that you have FOR yourself."* You can only love your neighbor in the way that you love yourself. If we want to become mature believers and move beyond spiritual milk, we have to understand and dive into loving ourselves and not being ashamed or feeling guilty about doing so. This book is comprised of 51 ways that I found to loving myself in my darkest hours that built me back to a place of peace with God and myself. Affirming that I had to walk with God instead of just including Him in my WILL and asking him along for the ride. The most important thing to remember is we are going to face hills and valleys. The worse possible way of dealing with the ups and the downs is to avoid them because it is the unknown or we are scared. With strength and courage, walk straight into the EYE of the storm of your fears and He will sustain you through them through His promise, *"Yea, though I walk through the valley of the shadow of death, I will fear no evil: for thou art with me; thy rod and thy staff they comfort me..."* This book helped me during my hardest times of transitions, and from one friend to another—you will make it through, God will use this time to mature you to find your love in ONLY Him and not be dependent upon outside sources to make you feel fulfilled. If you take this book seriously and practice what is in it, it will help launch you into a place where you experience a deep sense of understanding, loving who you are in our Father. The suggested reading strategy for *51 Ways to eXpress Love to Yourself* is best read in weeks as opposed to days (yet you are free to read it in whatever way best suits your needs.) Every lesson should be taken as one week concept to flesh out alongside answering questions that can be scattered throughout the week to keep your mind stayed on the changes you are bringing about through awareness. Most of us can read fast – and in this consumption culture, we fit in, yet I find comprehension usually takes longer. That said, please do not rush the process- take it week by week, slowly. Change can happen instantly, but long term change usually occurs slowly and over a period of time. Additionally think about the purpose intended - we all know, there are 52 weeks in a year, yet there are 51 lessons...Why might you ask? That 52nd week is for YOU to establish what you learned – your most valuable lesson and your responsibility to bringing about the changes you seek in your life, from your soul. Plainly put – change takes time – pace yourself and have grace (and room) for your growth.

Thank you for taking the time to read and thank you for loving yourself enough to purchase this book and change your own life for God's glory!

1.) Ground Yourself in Something That is Rooted - By Yourself (Psalm1:3)

Life can be downright crazy! Sometimes the winds of life will blow so viciously you have to be planted in something consistent to stay put. Consider a tree firmly planted in the ground by the roots - when the winds come, a few branches might break off, but the winds do not have permission to uproot the tree IF its roots reach deep enough in the ground. So, what does that mean for us? It means we ought to take the time to establish our roots so that we too can become grounded, unmovable individuals, like a tree. When the winds of life come (and rest assured they will), find something that you can be deeply rooted in. For me, what keeps me grounded is quiet time in the word of God. If all else goes wrong in the day, morning, or night, I know that I can count on those thirty minutes to acknowledge my inner peace and give me comfort because my routine is something I have taken years to form and is not easily negated by stress, heartache, or problems (aka the winds of life). For others, "rooting" could look like an activity - such as yoga, adventure (making intentional space to be in nature or city to explore), or acts of service (taking time to volunteer).

Whatever activity you chose to do, make it consistent and a steady practice that becomes so familiar it is akin to breathing. The reason why we ought to do this is it will help us establish a consistent form when life becomes hectic around us. We don't have to submit ourselves to the chaos that life will sometimes bring. When all else fails, you can be found in the consistency of routines that make you feel invigorated, confident, and refreshed because it is unchanging. Ground yourself—you'll need it to take flight.

❖ What activity will you be committed to be rooted in for the days of this month? (Scientifically, research has shown it takes 21 days of consistency to form a habit.)

❖ How do you think this will help you grow as a person to love yourself more?

❖ What does it mean to be rooted "in" something?
(In your own words)

2.) Be Your Own Biggest Cheerleader (Philippians 4:13)

Honestly speaking, I was down in the dumps, and after the crowd dissipated from my life, I had no one to spur me on through my deep depression. It was evident that I had learned how to survive from the praises of men, and when the chants were removed, I crumbled. The truth is, as long as others were cheering for me, I was empowered. It dawned on me that while I appeared confident, I never knew how to bolster that same confidence for myself, by myself. It was in these specific times when I had to reestablish how to find encouragement within me. If all your life people gas you up, one day you'll arrive at the gas station and wonder what to do. I was allowing myself to be serviced and never accountable to servicing myself. We must LEARN how to support ourselves with or without the crowd. As Lacrae says, "If you live for others' acceptance, you'll die from their rejection." Now, when I say be your own biggest cheerleader, I do not mean in a vain or conceited way. I mean be accountable to the fact that you were put on this earth with a unique purpose in mind and celebrate that in you! Take a football game for example; it's about the bigger picture. When cheerleading is done right, the cheerleaders/fans pump up the football players, which then fuels the spirits of the entire team to win! Consider yourself to be the cheerleader, the football team, the fans, and the bus, driving yourself to the goals you want to meet in your life to win! Walk with your head held up knowing you are Kings and Queens of the Most High! Give yourself compliments, write encouraging notes on your bathroom mirror, but whatever you do—never stop cheering for your dreams and desires. At some points in life, it may be the only voice that you hear, so take the time to make sure it is MATURE, LOUD, and UNWAVERING!

❖ List 3 specific ways you will begin to encourage yourself this week?

❖ What are some of the best compliments you have heard repeated about yourself throughout your life? (Write at least three.) Do you believe them when they were said?

❖ Is it hard for you to believe you are worth everything that you give and say to others? If no, why? If yes, how can that expand even more?

3.) Know How Valuable Your Time is and Let it Not Be Filled with Busy Business (Luke 10:38-42)

Could you imagine holding space with one of the greatest influencers in the world? I mean, really picture it; an iconic hero/streamer/ Tik-Tok-er sitting right in front of you and you have the unique opportunity to have a three-hour session with him/her; one on one. What would you do? What would you ask? How would you handle the situation? What's funny is we always have access to enter the throne room of grace with our heavenly Father. We don't have to "imagine" yet we find that when we actually have the time to approach God, we flat out don't, or we are easily distracted sitting in His presence, believing advancement in the world is far more important than advancing in the spiritual realm. This is a lie. Your spirit is connected to everything you do and informs every decision made. This is a tale as old as time, and we see it illustrated in the book of Matthew with two sisters; Mary and Martha. This is a classic case of quantity versus quality time; busy work versus purposed work, and you are going to need to know the difference between each if you intend to live a purposeful life. Allow me to let you in on a truth—God isn't pleased when we do "busy" work for the kingdom, God does not NEED us to do anything, He is God and can do anything He wants; however, He chooses us. We are a chosen people. That should change the way we look at our lives. How we view quality time spent will determine the fruit which springs forth from our lives. His heart's desire is for our work to be purposed and peaceful. Think of the work of Martha and Mary and who Jesus was pleased with. Mary knew the value of the moment in front of her and because of that did what was "right" in the eyes of Yeshua; for service is not to earn love but should be propelled from a heart of thanksgiving, not obligation. Busyness makes us a slave to obligation, choosing allows us options and autonomy. My encouragement to you? Value God, family, work, and friend time and protect it with swift diligence from the distraction that busyness can sometimes bring.

❖ What is the difference between busyness and purposed work?

❖ How do you feel when you know the work you are doing is purposed with a mission?

❖ What are indicators of busy work in your own life? Describe how you feel after busy work in full length.

4.) Be 100% Honest with Yourself Before Others HAVE to Be (Proverbs 12:22)

Honesty is a virtue that is one of the greatest assets we can offer one another as human beings. Without honesty, truth can never be uncovered and growth will never take place. Over time, I have realized when I was in my worst seasons of life I was in that place only because of my own actions toward my family, friends, church, community, and, worse—actions against myself. It takes a certain humility to take an honest look at the mistakes that we make in our own lives that put us in a less than desirable position. In our flesh, we can be certain we will make mistakes, and even though we are covered by His grace, we will have to face the consequences for our sinful nature in this lifetime. Be mindful and honest about where you are, but have enough faith to know that even if it is "negative," at the time, you won't stay there- God will not leave you there! If you are facing addiction, be brave enough to bring it to the Father and to a loving, trustworthy person who can offer help. If you are not the nicest person to others, take steps to be kinder to those around you in small, significant ways.

If you are lost and confused, admit it and find the direction you wish to go, seeking wise counsel and knowledge. The true issue arises when we see the elephant in the room and refuse to do anything in response when we know we ought to. If you struggle with honesty with yourself, be bold enough to ask a trusted confidant, "What do you see in my life that reflects goodness? What message do I put out in the world by my presence, good or bad?" This will certainly take maturity and you have to let you guard down to listen, but sometimes it is better to swallow a bitter pill in private from a loved one then to be humiliated in the public eye by someone who cares nothing for you. Be honest with yourself before life has to.

❖ What is your elephant in the room you have yet to deal with in honesty?

❖ Have you considered reaching out for help in this
   area of life? (Why or why not?)

❖ What is the first step you are going to take to help solve this issue?

5.) Guard Your Greatest Asset (Proverbs 4:23)

"Above all else, guard your heart, for everything you do flows from it."

I never understood this gem until God allowed an unprecedented amount of hurt and pain to happen to me in order help me understand. Because we are Kingdom subjects, what we allow IN is what we push out; we are sponges and will bleed our surroundings from our spirits. You should be cautious about who and what you allow in your life space, for it is a sacred gift from God and essentially your ministry. With a wounded and beaten heart, it is incredibly difficult to love and even harder to trust people. Do not allow others to set up war ground on the battlefield that is your heart, and you do that by guarding it. How do we guard it? Prayer and wisdom. Look, I'm going to be straight up—some personal information is sacred and therefore should only be trusted with a select few. Allow trust to be earned before giving up the secret garden of your heart. Be aware of allowing every influence in your life into your home space. Be mindful of the company you keep; proverbs says, *"a companion of fools suffers harm,"* and there is a GOOD reason behind that.

In our walk, if we learn how to trust God at His word, guarding the very gift that He has given us (our hearts), He won't have to needlessly repair the broken parts that we have given to pursuits lesser than our true calling. This does not mean we should live in a conservative Christian bubble, for then we cannot be effective for the Kingdom. Setting healthy boundaries for yourself ensures you are okay and it also covers those whom you minster to or have friendships with. Guard your heart and it will flow with the solutions of life, not the problems!

❖ In what ways have you done a good job in guarding you heart?

❖ In what ways can you do a better job at guarding your heart?

❖ Have you ever had a feeling you weren't supposed to do something, and you did it anyway and the end result turned out bad? What lesson did you learn about guarding your heart?

6.) Detach From the Rat Race (Matthew 6:22-23)

It is so easy to get caught up in the rat race that is life sometimes. In this day and age, we have made an idol of social media, and while it has helped in a plethora of ways it has also damaged the very essence of what I like to call the "now" of the moment. You see, social media can take you everywhere, all at once, while you miss the present moment happening right in front of you. Social media is one HUGE rat race where people can fabricate their lives to appear more glamorous than they actually are. One has to remember, because we are people of fallen nature with (sometimes) inflated egos, we always tend to highlight the best parts of our lives while leaving the worst parts off the camera roll and out of sight. To have a realistic view of your life, sometimes you have to put down the candy, mature, and eat food. This means, live life outside the lens of your camera or a status update every now and again. Be okay with leaving your phone at home (fasting from it can help as well) and/or just taking a break from social media accounts altogether. All those accounts will be there when you return, and the time away will help you be present in what God is doing in the now.

This way, we can stop comparing and contrasting our lives with others and tune in to what we have in front of us. Being present is a gift, so give it to yourself and others by taking a break and detaching from the race. I did this myself; not for a day, not for a month, but an entire year. I went without a phone, and it was liberating! What I learned is three things. 1.) Being present is a skill. You cannot imagine how much I noticed when I didn't have a phone in front of me how people struggled to keep eye contact or were constantly fidgeting with their pockets. You will literally up your communication skillset simply by not being interrupted in the flow of conversations. 2.) If people love you and truly care about you, they will find a way to contact you; this is how you know who your circle is. When I fell off the face of the planet, a few people called my wife looking for me in order to talk to me because I was checked out! People began to reach out to me on social media and waited for my reply via computer! What I am saying is sometimes we have space fillers and detaching lets us know who needs to be a priority and who needs to stay grouped with the majority. 3.) Undistracted, you have so much time to focus on your purpose, execute your mission, and work hard at it without stopping or getting lost on a feed. Basically sometimes it's good to be able to unplug to tune in!

❖ How do you feel regarding your friends and their accomplishments they post on social media? By comparison, do you sometimes feel behind or ahead?

❖ How do you think fasting from social media might help you personally?

❖ (Assuming you will) What did you learn after a week of fasting from social media?

7.) Don't Try to Keep Up with The Jones', Because They are in a Different Game (Galatians 6:4)

With the invention of social media (as discussed in the previous point) it is so easy to become distracted by the lives of others. No matter how hard we try, we find ourselves not only watching but trying to keep up with the Jones'. A conversation in our head sounds something like, "The Jones' created a new business. The Jones' bought a new car. The Jones' bought a new home. The Jones' children made a 4.0 and are on the dean's list. The voice of discouragement creeps in, which sounds something like, "What exactly is taking place in *my* life that's so great?" The interesting contrast to the Jones's is while you are watching them, they are watching their lives, and the best thing that you can do is keep your eyes on the road God has assigned you to. You should work hard but out of pure dedication and passion, not from competition and jealousy. When we are driven from those places (jealousy and competition) it produces unhealthy behaviors because it is a non-sustainable fuel that gives no gas to our lives.

When you have a dream, be sure to make it **rooted** to your divine purpose in life and not rooted in others' accomplishments in your field of work. Besides, when comparing your results to another, it strips the joy away from the very things you have accomplished and the sheer process it took getting there. Keep focused on your road and watch where God will take you!

❖ How does keeping up with the Jones' effect your joy specifically?

❖ Do you take time to celebrate your own accomplishments? If yes, how? If no, why not? (I believe you should start today)

❖ What are 3 ways you prevent comparison from happening in your life too often?

8.) Be Passion in Action (James 2:17)

God gives all of us passion concerning various pursuits of life, but to possess passion is one thing, to act on it another. Understand that when you desire something, desire is only part of the equation. The second part of the battle is to fight for it and know that hard work plus faith equals a desired outcome. For instance, let's say you like a woman; you can have passion all day, but until you walk up to that pretty fine thing and say, "Queen - I want you to be the ONE I put a ring on and make some children" without saying it you would NEVER get to experience that woman, because passion is only part of the dream; it's the ACTION that makes the vision complete. Simply put, you are bringing life to your vision when you supplement it with action. Now, because I am an artist, I am drawn to music, and when I hear it I'm going to share my gift and dance! Now, here is the thing, the moment always comes down to a choice, I can be passion in action by creating my moment or I can be passive and shrink because of my insecurities, my doubts, and fears. You have to learn how to actively pursue your passions. Remember, God even says *"to faith add works."* So, work at it and give it your all! If you have dreams, stop waiting on them to come to pass and be passion in action. Also, if you don't know where to go as far as direction, ask our heavenly Father and He will certainly give direction to you. He sounds like that still small voice moving you toward that dream in your heart that you have already been given before you were born! Be passion and be in action.

❖ What is something you have been waiting on God to do in your life?

❖ What are some things that might aid God in the vision that He has given you while waiting? (This could be building character, not giving up, taking classes, finding a mentor, etc.)

❖ What dream would you pursue if you knew you could not fail? (The answer you give now is the very thing that you should be pressing into.)

9.) Produce Endorphins and Release Dopamine to Make Your Heart Happy (Proverbs 17:22)

We all want to be happy, JOY filled people, and sometimes that is just not the case. We find ourselves wrestling somewhere in between barely making it and mountaintop experiences without balance. This constant inconsistency is not where God wants us to live, He built something within us that can help us achieve a stable level of constant joy. The human body does amazing things! The body naturally produces a high where you don't have to use drugs in order to obtain the high. You see, when you work out by running, jogging, or my personal favorite, dancing, your body produces dopamine. Basically, dopamine is serotonin and oxytocin, and the releasing of these chemicals sends messages to your neurotransmitters that cause endorphins to release—giving you happiness and joy instantaneously! God says, *"The joy of the Lord is my strength."* While it is a strength, joy can also be strategy to fight depression, sadness, and to keep yourself fit and full of life and vigor. All you have to do is become physically active, be sure to include that in your daily routine, and see how much happier you will be because of it. Becoming more fit helps boost an overall positive personal image. In this way, you get three benefits for the execution of exercising once. Think of happiness as a state of being, not a mood posture, then you will be able to create that feeling anytime you release activity into your life!

❖ Is working out a part of your daily routine? (If yes, GOOD, keep it that way. If no, what's stopping you from obtaining joy, health, and happiness?)

❖ If you answered, "I don't have time," my next question would be: is there any place you devote time that could be exchanged for exercise? We have twenty-four hours in a day, we can take at least one to improve our health, happiness, and self-image. If you don't have time to better yourself, you won't better yourself.

❖ Spend the next thirty minutes online searching the benefits of working out. If you know **why** something is important in truth, it brings more value to the issue, prompting extreme change. Fill yourself with truth and record your findings here!

10.) Be A Complimentary of People (Matthew 7:12)

Let's just be real, nowadays there is not too much to be "happy" about and we carry that burden with us. A ton of people, including myself at times walk around with sour faces and bad attitudes. Everyone dislikes it when they come into contact with those types of individuals, but as people we seldom ask "Why. Why don't people want to be around sour faces?" Now, some people you simply cannot help; they are devoted to be salty twenty-four-seven, but for the minority, nine times out of ten, the reason for their unpleasant ways isn't because they are actually that way but because their soul is not being fed and need a boost! We can chose to be that boost. The truth is if you are on the outside of faith, the world can become a very pessimistic, dark place, offering little to no hope when it comes to this chaotic thing we call life. Plainly put: life is hard, and sometimes people need a light shined on them to get through the hard times (in the same way you'll need it from time to time). That is where you and I come in. Give others light by finding little ways to build them up. Eventually, you will reap what you sow. Whatever you do, look for the best in people, and then tell them about their best. As my best friend Jason says is, "If you don't have anything nice to say, don't say it at all," but instead of the negative side of the perspective he encourages, "if you have something nice to say, you should say it." Don't waste time or spiritual energy gossiping or badmouthing God's other children, because we are all on the same playing field, whether we acknowledge Him or not. Besides, we are called to be encouragers. Whatever we speak in authority goes out of our mouths and either builds a kingdom atmosphere everywhere we go or destroys lives around us. So, compliment family members who display devout loyalty. Compliment that stranger's shoe game if they have on some fire sneakers or heels that are on fleek (for my people not familiar with slang, fire means good, not flames, fleek equals on point!). Boast freedom in those who are not yet free, because our words hold strength and power in them. In doing this, you will change cultures and environments and lift others up simultaneously.

❖ When do you find yourself giving out the most compliments? What are they usually for?

❖ Can you challenge yourself this week to give everyone you see or know a compliment? What have you really got to lose, and what may be the thing that stops you from doing so?

❖ How do you feel when you get a compliment for your clothes, personality, or your faith? (The Bible says do unto others as you would want done unto you.) How does that scripture affect how you think about lifting up others since you yourself want to be lifted?

11.) Invest in Yourself and ALWAYS Bet BIG (Proverbs 15:32)

"A man who spurns reproof abhors his own soul, but he that hears reproof has an understanding heart." There is a great reason why God mentions this in the Bible, because when people give good advice, we ought to do everything we can to take it and run with it! Not only should we take good, Godly advice, but we also need it to invest in who we are. A plant without water does not grow, and the same is true concerning advice without investment in self. In order for you, your business, your life, and spirit to grow, you must invest, recognizing opportunities as they come. If you want health, invest in working out, and go hard! If you want wealth, invest in finical advisors and conferences that will ignite wisdom and guidance towards wealth. If you want to live with purpose, serve and be mentored by leaders in your local church community or well-established nonprofit orgs. I want you to think of this one statement every time you feel yourself not wanting to seek wisdom to grow: "INvestments help the INner man." Do not allow your stock to drop by missing your blessing to choose; invest in yourself and risk big.

God's hands can and will catch you if you fall,
and He has been a faithful guide to His sheep.

❖ In what areas of life could you begin investing in yourself or betting big or by taking risk?

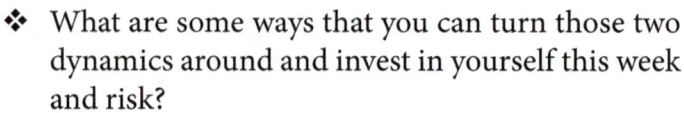

❖ What are some ways that you can turn those two dynamics around and invest in yourself this week and risk?

❖ What area in your life would you like to see the most growth in? What are you going to do to ensure that you will see that growth?

12.) Be Thankful for it All (Thessalonians 5:18)

They say that the only difference between a healthy attitude and an unhealthy attitude is the attribute of learned thankfulness. Think about it, if you are grateful for everything that comes your way, a world of infinite possibilities shows itself, because thankfulness is not based upon circumstance, it's a character-based virtue. Understanding the practice of gratitude allows everything to become an instant blessing. The upsets of life try to bring us down, but thankfulness transforms situations into setups for bigger blessings down the road. The author in 1st Thessalonians 5:8 gives an accurate description of what the posture of our hearts must look like in order to gain all that God has in store for us; he writes, *"In everything, give thanks, for this is the will of God in Christ Jesus concerning you."* Meaning, we never have to question the will of God because it starts and ends with a heart of gratitude. If you want to understand a life of following Christ and fulfilling your unique purpose, be humbly thankful for everything that comes your way; good or bad. Through this lens, we'll start to view challenges not as negative obstacles but as opportunities to help us handle situations with more maturity and to preserve the best versions of ourselves in Christ!

❖ Where do you find yourself most disappointed in life currently with an unexpected outcome to a hopeful start of a situation?

❖ What is your detailed plan to see the blessing through the trial?

❖ In the long term, what effects can an ungrateful heart have on your life?

13.) Be Around the Likeminded (Proverbs 13:20)

Picture you have a group of "friends," of which none are interested in what you personally like to do. Oh, it would painful/isolating to hang out with people who do not share common interest, goals, or ideas, yet to fit in we sometimes subject ourselves to people who are nowhere near our level of maturity, growth, or development for many reasons. Amid this lack of challenge, we find ourselves stuck and frustrated, not moving along but frozen in time, and then have the nerve to ask ourselves, "How SWAY?!" Well, like Kayne proclaimed in a feisty interview, we find we too do not have the answers as to why we have become stagnant; I'll save you time; it's our circle of influence. There are times in life where you must move forward; after all, God is a progressive God who takes charge of everything; past, present, and future. It is important to realize that when God is moving you toward your calling, you surround yourself with friends and family of the same mindset. Why? Like mindedness will always serve the highest common goal together. If you are not of the same mindset, it will produce stagnancy, conflict, or even worse, back-sliding into past moments and emotions already lived/experienced.

If you really want to change the course of history, be around those who also desire a change as well.

❖ As soon as you read this, I'm certain 1-3 people came to mind, my question is why have you not let them go yet?

❖ What is the root of why you feel you cannot live life without those people? Maybe it is a deep sense of fear, maybe it's because they are all you have ever known, maybe it's because they say you won't find better friends, but it's important to discover WHY you feel you cannot live without them and destroy that, because the only thing you truly need is GOD, for He is more than enough and He will bring new friends or family to aid you in your purpose if asked.

❖ How do you feel when you are on the "outside" of the friendship looking in? Will you take a stand to see your value and dive into relationships that can support you and your visions?

14.) Readers Digest: The Menu: Passion, Challenge, and Beyond (Proverbs 1:5)

One thing I have learned in my youth is that School House Rock never lied when it made the statement "Knowledge is Power." So much of who we derives from what we absorb through our primary senses. One thing that promotes rapid growth and progress is learning, and the conduit I personally favor is reading. There is a plethora of books out there, from A-Z, so what should, or do we read? Well, let me introduce you to PCB. The PCB method is one that REALLY works. When picking material to read, I suggest reading three types of books. **Passion reads**; books/magazines/ articles that highlight, inform, and direct you deeper into your interest, hobbies, and/or occupation. These "passion" books should give you new perspectives and thoughts on the things you already love. The next type of books are **challenge reads**; maybe these materials are a stretch for your vocabulary or the ideas presented are a bit out of reach conceptually… read it anyway so that it will put you in a position of being uncomfortable and you are reaching for new heights of wisdom and knowledge; looking up words and having to use a search engine for every page read. Trust that the growth will be exponential, even though the read might prove tough at first. The last and final material is **beyond reads**; read material that is beyond where you live, eat, or places you have gone or know of. It will build a vision for all the places you can go, things you can accomplish, and the person you aspire to be by the time you get there!

❖ Are you an avid reader right now? What stops you from picking up books or podcasts and diving into them? (Distractions, importance, lack of value.)

❖ Some of us just do not like to read, and that is okay. The future of tech has brought us to the video age where just about anything we need to know can be found online in video format. Video is the new book of 2022 and beyond. How will you apply this same principle to video this week? What videos are you going to search for with the PCB method?

❖ You are what you eat. What most people do not realize is a lot of people are full of reality tv, gossip, and social junk food. What are you full of and how will that change in time?

15.) Improve Lifestyle Through Mentorship (Proverbs 11:14)

No one man or woman has it ALL figured out, and if we truly feel that way, we struggle with pride. When we try to figure out everything, we usually end up making a ton of mistakes and then end up living in regret or reviewing the past through the lens of bad choices and mistakes. Mentors are a great way to help us see mistakes before we make them because of their life experience having navigated roads before us. They should be qualified enough to see the hole before we ever step foot in it. There are several mentor types too; business, spiritual, life, and all are needed to help with growth to improve the quality of our lives. Search for mentors who are individuals you look up to and are in a high position of influence with good character. I do not care how big their profile is, if there character is trash – it won't be long before it falls. I'll be honest, it takes humility to be underneath someone, so also understand that respect and honor to your mentor goes a long way. No one desires to pour out their entire life to a student who doesn't give back or who doesn't display a teachable heart. Just how would you give back to a mentor and display humility? You give credit where credit is due when you are successful through their teaching. You thank them for their time and resources that helped put you in a position to grow regardless of their posture. Understand that they are human and make mistakes and always, always, always point people in the direction of where your understanding has come from. If you follow the format of how to grow underneath leadership, God in no time will establish a flock underneath you someday. Think about the biblical superhero David. He was underneath an incompetent leader (Saul) for what seemed like years, was more qualified and was obedient to the call of God; yet he didn't allow his ego to supersede that which was God's plan to build him up in character and integrity before His kingdom was given to him. Be like David, know your place, understand who you are, and grow through mentorship.

❖ When I was younger, I felt mentorship was silly, but as a young man I realized I needed it more than I thought. Do you struggle with the idea of finding a mentor? Do you feel it makes you appear weak?

❖ What are some pros to finding a mentor in your field of passion? What advantages can you list out in the space below?

❖ A mentor is defined as a trusted and experienced advisor. Think of the men and women in your life and write down three that you trust and that are experienced in the field you are attempting to grow in, and purse them; ask for them to mentor you in some form. By the end of the week, you should have three mentors in your life who are consistent and want to see your success! GO and find them!

16.) Do Not Be Afraid of Failure (Joshua 1:9)

Fear is the greatest emotion that inhibits advancement in all our lives. Those doubtful voices, "What if I can't. How will I live if it doesn't turn out the way I planned? What if the vision never comes to pass?" However, if we succumb to fear and its constructs; eventually, it will turn into its nastier cousins—regret and guilt. Regret because we did not do when we could have and guilt because maybe if we would have acted in love and passion, we might have accomplished what we set out to do. Failure can teach you many things, yet its two greatest lessons are these: how much determination do you really have, and do you really want the desired goal you are chasing? Anything worth having requires hard work, and the truth is you'll never get the answer to either of the questions until you are no longer fearful of failure. Get off your biscuit and risk it. On the other side of that fear is the greatest reward—courage to start the process all over again. Life is linear. What most of us fail to realize is that with every failure, we still move forward, because we must. Life won't reverse itself if we mess up and fail, and it's just more evidence that even if we do fail, we are always failing forward.

The only difference is we can fail forward and go up or we can fail forward and go down, but one thing is certain; we cannot do both. Do not end your life with ideas that were million-dollar ideas. Do not think of a bestselling novel yet it never discovers the light of day to be published or written. Failure is just a prideful heart without understanding. See failure as a process and not product and each failure will turn into a lesson!

❖ "You are only a failure if you give up." If that was your new mantra, how would that change the way you view failures in your own life?

❖ Failure is inevitable. In honesty, everything is not going to turn out in your favor the way you would like it to, but if you see the lesson, you become wiser and more learned. What has a specific failure taught you about life?

❖ Failure is life's way of asking, "How committed are you?" What is your biggest vision in life and how committed are you to seeing it come to pass?

17.) Learn How to Change Your Emotional State (Romans 12:2)

We are not super humans, as much as we would like to believe. We sometimes run low on gas and need a good release. Tony Robins (one of my book mentors) says, "experience your emotions, but never stay in the state concerning negative ones." For example, it is okay to feel sad and express it to a family member or a friend, but do not let yourself remain in a perpetual state of sadness or any one emotion for that matter. One exercise you can do to change your state is to express your feeling through arts such as dancing or singing. You can change your state by going out for a run by the lake. Another way to alter your state of mind is to take all of the emotions felt and put them into something productive. You must learn how to direct your feelings and gain mastery of where to place them. Changing your state is as simple as not dwelling on something negative after it is said and done; its allowing time for process but when it becomes too much to bear putting the issue down and allowing it to breathe a little. Changing your state is a cognitive choice; knowing what plagues you but operating in a spirit of hope and focusing on what's right in your life. There is always beauty in the struggle, because it's all a part of the process. Learn how to isolate the beauty of the time and learn how not to inflate or give more weight to the trials than necessary.

❖ What is something that took place this week that you still have the opportunity to change your state mind of about?

❖ Can you recall a time where you did not change your state after an argument or conflict and the feelings lingered and it affected you? How did this impact you and others around you?

❖ List three ways you can change your state (the next time you get into a jam, you can try these things).

18.) Cut Off Branches That Do Not Produce Fruit (John 15:2)

Have you ever been waiting for something/someone to come around after trying, season after season? Maybe it is a family member or a friend who has repeatedly hurt you and you are waiting for them to change? Or maybe it is the work from a job that feels like it is robbing you of all your joy and peace until you are downright unhappy. There is an anointed time and season for everything under the sun… The book of Ecclesiastes states, *"there is a time to search for and a time to give up."* The fact that you are connected to the Father is assurance that you will produce fruit, it's a blessing under the covenant of Christ; therefore, the expectation should be anyone you are around (in closeness as far as relationally) should produce fruit as well. And if that very sentiment is the expectation, think about when everyone comes together from your camp… it will be a beautiful, bountiful harvest! If you see any area of your life that is not producing fruit after constant effort, energy, and prayer; maybe God is saying it's time to cut the branches. Learn to cut the fat, especially if it is not needed in your daily diet. At times this could be gossip, slander- negative self-talk- showing up or pulling back from a friend group – whatever it might be, if it is not serving you and it will not be served, you need to cut it (just like the song).

❖ What are some things (whether occupation, friendship, or ideas) that are not producing fruit in your life?

❖ What insecurities do you have about cutting ties with what is listed above?

19.) Never Avoid the Woods in Your Work (Psalm 23:4)

When you are being drawn out into the wilderness of your life by faith, never avoid it—charge straight into it. This wilderness can be an emotional wilderness, a career wilderness, a health wilderness, a family and friend wilderness... What is wilderness? A wilderness is where you walk into the truest form of who you actually are and not the ideas that you convey and try to maintain this posture on a day-to-day basis. The wilderness is where you become stripped of the false pretenses that you sometimes hide behind because the pressures of life haven't yet tested the fragile personality that just can't hold up against the hammer of life called pain and its twin sister reality. The wilderness is the RAWest part of spiritual WARfare, and God is the only thing holding you up because everything else has left. Remember the Israelites were God's chosen people, but God drawing them out of Egypt was with the intention of breaking the mental bondage and slave mentality that could've held them back in the promised land (if the old ways were carried over with them). To love yourself, you have to know the truest version of who you are, and the wilderness always will bring that out because no one else is around; it is just you, God, and the crickets. He will work in all-times, but the wilderness is distraction free, it's our place where we can hear Him speak above all the noise in our life. Center yourself and walk into the woods fearlessly.

❖ Have you ever been brought to the woods of your life, right on the edge of them by God, and turned away because you knew it meant sacrificing pride or giving up something that you wanted? Instead of entering the woods in obedience, you overcompensated with more work and buried the call? If no, are you in the woods currently struggling? How does it make you feel?

❖ Did you ever take the time to realize that in the wilderness (concerning biblical heroes) is where God takes that time to shape, inform, and make prophets better than they were BEFORE they entered? Moses led God's people from Egypt after his stint in the woods. Jonah after being swallowed by the whale saved an entire nation from being wiped away by the wrath of God, calling them to repentance. Christ, after the Garden of Gethsemane, took the cross, endured the wilderness of death, and came back resurrected. How does that make you feel about the wilderness you will soon encounter or are already in?

❖ How can going into the wildness or experiencing the wilderness make you a stronger man or woman?

20.) Listen to Good Music

There are a lot of tunes out there nowadays. With the invention of various streaming sites, anyone with a microphone, a thought, and a simple app can record music. BUT we find out very quickly that not all of the music out is GOOD music. Good music inspires, lifts up, informs, and transforms your model of thinking, it helps shift your mood. With that being said, the music you are currently listening to; does it lift you up or pull you down into misery and low vibe thoughts? Does it remind you of times past that were not so good or does it spark a wonderful interest in the future and inspire new motion? We must remember Satan was the King and officiate of music in heaven and what we entertain through music is essentially his dwelling place on this kingdom of earth. We ought to be wary of music that popularizes and romanticizes ideas we do not want in our own lives. Most music these days is used as novelty, junk food if you will – even the way it is produced, but we need to get back to seeing music as a pathway to joy and peace. This cannot be achieved by seeking out distasteful and non-inspired music.

❖ What music are you currently playing through your speakers?

❖ How have you seen Satan in today's musical influence? What is at the edge of your generations sound? (What is being talked about and where do you resonate with it, honestly?)

❖ How can you safeguard your spirit from the popular culture that is the music industry and mainstream music?

21.) Rest – Rest – Rest (Genesis 2:2)

In the technological age, everything moves so quickly. In fact, time, space, and people move so quickly rest hardly seems like a priority anymore; however, rest is (or should be) a priority, it is essential to loving yourself. For example, I mentored a college dance student who suffered a concussion from dancing and was having issues focusing in school and rehearsals. Although her body and mental space was not up to functional standards, she pushed herself amidst her overall wellness until I intervened and told her, "yes, all of these things are important (school, work, rehearsals, etc.), but when it's all said and done, your teachers, friends, and cohorts will not be in the hospital with you if and when you go down from pushing yourself beyond what you can actually accomplish. The same people who will push you to crash out, won't be there when you do and that is important to know regarding self-care. I always tell my wife; you cannot serve effectively at 50%, and no matter how much people want you to, it is up to you to set boundaries and take time to take a break, even when it isn't extreme conditions – like a concussion. Even if it is finding one day each week to tune out emails, cellphones, and people. You will be far more productive when you do come back to your work, instead of being "tired busy." When we allow ourselves to rest, we are giving space for us to recognize that while we are not little g - god.

❖ On a scale of 1-10 where are you at in your stress level (10 being the worse amount of stress and 1 being the lower side of stress)? If your level is five or higher, what is causing your stress? And if lower than five, how do you maintain such a level head while everything is going on and how has that attitude helped others?

❖ What are some things listed above that you can monitor to ensure that you are getting adequate rest for the hours of work you are putting in?

❖ Do you believe rest should be held in the same importance that productivity is?

22.) Give Back
(Acts 20:35)

God says, "*it is better to give than it is to receive,*" because giving is only an extension of what God blesses His children to have in the first place. While it is a gift to give, one thing that often goes unsaid is to use wisdom and discernment when giving. Too often the ideology is held that you should give without parameters because that is what believers do but understand that there is a fine line between giving and being used up and taken advantage of. You cannot give anything you do not actually have or can afford not to have. God says, when you give, don't expect anything back. The gift is in the giving; the idea that you are meeting the needs of one of God's children. When you GIVE to others, you give it to yourself. The part of yourself that really needed it at a time and someone gave it to you freely. It's easy to objectify giving, yet I know in God's love, we are one. There is no measure of people in need of love and grace. You can give time, money, and an ear or volunteer a service. Get creative, but whatever you do, **give with a happy heart**—nothing will make you feel better and please God more than a cheerful giver!

❖ In what ways do you plan to give back today?

❖ Fully describe a time where you gave something (from the right place and posture) and how it made you feel.

❖ In the world, it is said that when giving you are losing something, but we find God's kingdom it is reversed; Christ says you are gaining something. Why do you think God counts it as a blessing to give more than it is to receive?

23.) Mediate Daily (Psalm 1:2)

Maybe you believe in God, maybe you don't, but what I do each morning is take time with God and talk to Him on a personal level. Sometimes, I can hear him well and sometimes I wonder if it is just my own voice in my head - I'll be honest. In the time I speak with Him, I tell Him thank you for another day, thank you for my wife, thank you for my daughter, and thank you for a purposeful work and a covering over my family with a hedge of protection. These mediations excite me, focus my mind to be thankful and look on the brighter side of why I do what I do. Next, I begin to clear out my worries and my stresses, asking God to help me in the areas where I need it most. After a certain point in time, I begin to see how small I really am and how big God is. I also take a certain amount of time to visualize. We are sensual beings – meaning we process life through our senses, so when I am taking time to envision myself in the current and future, I am building a healthier self-image. In my meditations I go in - my beard is full, my family is smiling, my muscles are toned. I am a millionaire in spirit and in my bank account too - I love God and the people He sent to my life and better they love me as well! I see what I desire and take small steps towards them daily, so when it does happen, it feels more like Deja-vu because I have witnessed the vision in my head so much. When I get done meditating, I feel a certain peace come over me. I say that to encourage you to find a routine where you can clear your head for ten minutes, talk yourself up, and focus your trajectory for the day to get in the zone so that you can have a productive, powerful day!

❖ There are taboos about meditation; "Those who meditate are weird and hippies, not spiritual," but it is so far from being true. What do you feel about meditation in general, and have you ever tried it in your life?

❖ What are some benefits of meditation?

❖ Will you attempt to meditate tonight? Write the experience down below.

24.) Let Go of the Past (Philippians 3:13)

Do you realize how much energy we expend replaying a film in our minds over the things that we could've, would've, or should've done? Paul says, *"He presses ahead, **forgetting** what is behind him,"* so why did he say that? The reason why is he (Paul) understood that dwelling on the past, mistakes, friendships, and relationships is not what truly matters in this lifetime. Take it from me, Paul should've been the one grieving because of shame and guilt from decisions prior to accepting Christ; after all, before he was appointed head of the church and a prolific writer of the New Testament (or majority of it), he was persecuting fellow Christians and killing the folks who were most associated with Christ. WHAT A GRACE TO BE PAUL! If anyone knows about having a terrible past, it is Paul, yet even he realizes that the past is not what matters! What matters is what God is doing NOW, and if you find yourself in a rut and stuck, it's simply because you need to move on from the good old days and get into your best days, which lie ahead of you. You cannot progress your story when you keep re-reading the last chapter. Let go of whatever was in your past that no longer serves the person you are growing to become.

It might be tough, even awkward at first because of the emotional ties, but once you release it fully, God can give you something that is more suited for the NOW.

❖ What are some things from your past that you just cannot seem to shake off of you?

❖ When it comes to the past, sometimes we allow it to linger because inadvertently we desire to be there in some capacity. Or we believe that if we think about it just one more time, we will discover why things went the way they went. We become detectives, scoping the scene of our lives and coming up short every time without good reason. Once I figured this out, it helped me so much; we cannot stop ourselves from thinking about the past, but we can determine how much time we spend focused on it. What are some habits that aid your past by being entertained? For example, maybe you listen to that song that reminds you of a painful breakup or revisit that IG page you shouldn't. Whatever it is, we want to eliminate things that trigger bad memories and limit our time in that area. Write triggers that make you go back to the past below.

❖ There is a difference in letting go of your past and facing it. Sometimes we **need to face our past.** Also, we might need help facing our past so that we can move on, and it is not as easy as just letting it go. We might just need the help of outside professionals, church counseling, or a trusted friend. Are there any problems regarding your past that you cannot let go of because of the damage it has done, and would you be willing to seek professional help to help sort through it? In a sense, help can seem taboo, you do not want to appear crazy or like one of those people in the movies, but the truth is everyone needs a supportive hand at moments. Remember, God says, *"Pride comes before the fall."* You do not want to miss the blessing of freedom because of pride. If you need help, seek it out, and you'll be better off because of it.

25.) Reward Yourself for Actually Doing Something (Colossians 3:23-24)

One thing that helped me break many addictive/negative behaviors is knowing the key behind breaking the habits. When it comes to setting goals and achieving them, the most important stages are planning and execution. This issue with unhealthy addiction overall is the instant gratification it provides in conjunction with our reward systems inside of our brains. You can shortcut your neurotransmitters to accept "shortcuts" by using drugs, alcohol, and substances to produce the happy chemical dopamine, but this fails ultimately because you are getting something for nothing. This is why addiction occurs; it is the desire to be happy without physical or mental stimulation. Research proves that the more you dabble with instant gratification methods the worse addiction becomes and the more you'll need substances to accomplish the "happy high." What I am offering is doing something that triggers that same response but in a less harmful way. The alternative? Set real-life trackable goals that create a sense of purpose and responsibility. Being productive is the new shortcut to happiness because it requires work, and your system will gain so much more from the goal being accomplished. A goal could be, to lose weight through dieting and exercise. Another goal could be to take a trip across the world like you always wanted to. The dream could be as simple as a swear jar to help your language, but the point is to have **trackable** goals to help create a sense of growth and progress. Begin to go for a lifestyle that peruses various goals that will lead to fulfillment (not success,) because the same neurons fire off when you go to take a swig from the bottle as when you achieve a goal (the more difficult the goal, the higher the fire)!

❖ What destructive habits do you attempt to reward yourself with? It doesn't have to be substance abuse either, it can be overeating, sweets addiction (like myself), over-working etc.

❖ Do these habits contribute to your overall wellbeing?

❖ Oftentimes people who have stolen will always go back to stealing if they have nothing to do with their hands. What is your POA (plan of action) to replace harmful habits with methods that prove productive, useful, and helpful? I suggest starting small – you do not need to change everything **just change that one habit for now.**

26.) Visualize Then Execute (Proverbs 16:3)

Do you know how close all of us are to obtaining our God-given dreams? Do you know what stops most of us from doing that very thing we were placed on this earth to do?

One step.

We dream these wonderful ideas; ideas that will change the world, ideas that could make us into who we know we are created to be, but we do not execute and take that first step. Truthfully, most of our amazing ideas will end up being shelved in the empty spaces of our head and we are reminded of them only when we see someone else succeeding in the very thing we once compulsively thought about. Not anymore. That changes with one faithful step today. Once we take one step, we take another and another and another until we are simply walking in our calling, and that is where we want to be! Visualize the life you always wanted and then take a step toward it. Don't think in huge chunks, break it down into smaller pieces. You want to be a streamer, create a page day 1. Day 2 record a video for said page. Day 3 upload video to said page and start all over again. One step per day = becoming.

I promise you, with consistency and hard work, you will achieve something intangible – becoming.

❖ What is one step that you have held off for too long in making the first move toward your destiny?

❖ Have you set up accountability to ensure that you make that first step?

❖ During your peak hours of solitude and meditation; I want you to begin painting a picture of the day you would like to have. Visualize your upbeat attitude, even when things go awry, visualize your success, things that will go right. Next, I want you to visualize where you will be, your friends at that time, how you look, what you are wearing, the car you are driving. While it hasn't come to pass, if you can see it, it is possible to achieve it. The first step is the visualization.

27.) Take Ownership and Know Your Role (Galatians 6:5)

Everyone has somewhat of an ideal blueprint to their lives. It is the idea of how life should be, what life could be, and the reality of what our lives are. Where most of us go wrong is we ask advice from family and friends (with good intentions). We then make choices based off the advice given; hate the results, and then play the blame game, not owning our part in making the decision. It is not that we shouldn't ask for advice, because the word says, *"A wise man will hear and increase in learning, and a man of understanding will acquire wise counsel,"* but we must take ownership of our choices, even when the results do not play out as previously envisioned. Also the key word is WISE, not Pookey from down the street or Ray-Ray on the corner. For advice to be taken seriously it must be from someone who produces fruit in the area you are looking to expand in. In total, this is your life. Never pawn off the responsibility of making choices and defining your destiny to family and friends' advice, because at the end of the day, as my father would always say, "If stuff goes left, you have to live with the consequences, not them!"

It still holds true to this day. Again, one life is all that is promised, you must learn to OWN who you are.

❖ How can you take ownership for your life today concerning your choices?

❖ When it comes to relationships, sometimes friends or spouses can be the scapegoat to our lack of vision or execution, causing tension in our relationship. Have you found yourself "playing the blame game" with those closest to you? How did it affect your relationship?

❖ What is the number one reason you haven't taken ownership for your life? Flush out the reasons.

28.) Choose the Right One (Ephesians 5:25)

Dating in 2017 has gotten so far away from what really matters in order to make a healthy relationship work. They have all these dating apps to connect the relationships and none to help maintain them. Social media has checkboxes that we can mark if they meet our criteria, but is that all that really matters - the outer being? Your height - weight – looks – skin color, is that all we are? Instead of focusing on only physical appearance, think about other things that are unchanging over-time. Think about a person's character. *Who* they are is what will eventually carry a relationship after looks and the outer shells crumble. Does this love interest support you? Do they show unconditional love, not only to you but to their family their friends? An even better question: do they show love even to their enemies? Do you share passions and interests on a deep, intimate level? Are your core values in the same department store? No one is perfect, and therefore, we should not expect it, but finding a spouse on the grounds of superficial traits such as looks, money, or a hot ride is a "model" of a relationship but fails to be one. Pray that God will lead you to him or her and He will stay true to His promise - in the same way he did for me.

❖ Choosing the right one doesn't mean that the person is a perfect fit, make no mistake; we are all flawed and broken, but the right one is anyone who is willing to grow, change, and learn from their past mistakes. How does knowing this take the pressure off making the wrong choice?

❖ How much do you believe the media influences your perception of what a good spouse is or should be? How does God's perspective influence your perception of what a good spouse is? (Compare and contrast.)

❖ The point of marriage is to establish a covenant between man and woman on earth, establishing what it looks like to die so that the other can live, just as Christ did for us. Knowing that; how does that affect what you look for in a person before dating or even marrying?

29.) When You Think About Giving Up, Remember Why You Started in the First Place (Hebrews 12:1-3)

Passion withers. As much as I hate to write these words on paper, sometimes we just do not feel motivated to press on; it's a defect of our limited human nature and at times, it's downright exhausting to press on when you are in a dark tunnel, searching for the light on the other side. Our feelings can sometimes confuse us until we grab hold of the reason we began our journey in the first place. I must constantly convince myself there is no better path than the one I have been set on, and there is gold waiting for me on the other side of the rainbow, but I can only collect my prize IF I remember the "WHY" attached to my journey. This life is to shape us, not break us. It is meant to teach us how to have a tough skin with a gentle heart. This life is given to us as a blank paper, and what we do with it, the color we add, the life we live, the people we touch, will be our masterpiece back to God. Is your WHY to provide for your family? Is your WHY to help free people from the bondage of mental slavery that has overtaken us all? Do you simply want to be used as a tool wherever humanity decides it has the most need? The key is to always ask yourself WHY, and if your reason is not compelling enough then keep brainstorming until you find a reason that is non-negotiable in your calling. Once you know why, the how is just the time before the big moment; why keeps you fueled between the moment and the process.

❖ When it comes to a very specific goal you have in life concerning a dream, WHY is it important to you?

❖ What are some of the extrinsic (motivations operating from outside) motivators that will help you remember why you are doing what you are doing? (Example: Getting a raise will help my family and give us a higher quality of life).

❖ What are some intrinsic (motivations operating from inside) motivators that can help you remember why you are doing what you are doing? (Example: Getting a promotion will make me feel more grounded because I have more responsibility, and I will use the challenge to build good character.)

30.) Help Others Along the Way—Key Phrase 'Along the Way' and Not Behind You (Galatians 6:7)

There are so many instances where people pray for the light to break through in their life. Maybe it's a business, it could be a simple hope for inspiration, or just a feeling of being overwhelmed with life; you just need a miracle to show up quick. Did you know you were put on this earth to be that breakthrough, to be the difference in one person's life that can ultimately change the course of their fate? A big shoe to wear, yet it's true! We can only love ourselves by ultimately realizing that we are the one we have been looking for our entire life. There is no separation with any of God's creation, because we are all connected! The Bible clearly states we reap everything we sow in this lifetime and in the next. We have to help others with due diligence because it helps us become all that God wants us to be, and that is beautiful. Yes, we all have priorities and things we need to get done; however, along our gracious journey, stop and aid someone else in their walk. You will find yourself more attuned to the idea that life isn't just about you but the collective experience through a greater connectedness to God in us.

❖ How can you help the person right next to you? If there is no one next to you, how are you going to serve the person you next see or talk to in the day? Would you be humble and willing to ask them if you can help them with anything and see what God can do in that moment? (It is okay if you do not neither, just write about what the thought of talking to a stranger makes you feel concerning faith.)

❖ How does the sentence "we are all connected" make you feel toward others? What does it say about how we should treat people if we are one in Christ with them?

❖ Why is it important to help those along the way versus behind you?

31.) Be Thankful for it All but Intentionally Choose the Small Things (Psalm 107:43)

My wife imparts deep wisdom in my life when I cannot seem to hear God for myself. One subject we constantly talk about is the big picture. I am always looking for the big bang of God, the red sea parting or manna falling from the sky, but as my wife so eloquently puts it, "it is a culmination of all the little things coming together that makes the big moment happen, and the real cool thing is; if we learn how to be thankful for those little occurrences that take place in our lives, we can enjoy the process instead of being full from just one moment. A moment that will be here today and gone tomorrow, fleeting. If we only look for the mountaintop experiences, then we have lost the amazing process through the valleys. There is adventure in the valley – do not lie to yourself! The moments you thought you could not power through but deep down you found the reserves to push on, do not tell me those don't carry an undisputed song in your heart. The transformations that took place rapidly while no one was watching. Be thankful for the small victories, the small gifts God arranges to give you, and the W's will show themselves left and right.

❖ What treasure that is small can you take a second and really appreciate and spend a minute being thankful for? Try and just sit in thanksgiving for as long as you can about whatever it is that you have in mind and write about it.

❖ What is a "valley of life," and what characteristics have you usually learned in your valleys in life?

❖ What will enjoying the small things do for your everyday living?

32.) Mistakes Do Not Define Your Life, They Make it Redeemable (Psalm 103:12)

People, throughout the course of history, often worry needlessly about the opinions of others. For all that they are worth, opinions do not count for much in the eyes of God, and they usually count most in conjunction with those who really know you. Like they say in the hood, "If you ain't paying my bills, don't worry about me and what I got goin!?" I believe this is how we should also consider the opinions of others we don't know concerning the mistakes we have made. There was a period in my life where I made a plethora of mistakes, almost too many to count within a year's time. I made so many mistakes; I didn't think I would ever see the light of day - only playing second fiddle to my pain and shame from those ill-advised moments. Then, I had a revelation; it's my story inspired in His glory. I needed to make mistakes to grow and see the true value of a grace that saves, forgives, and restores. However, let's just say I did live a perfect life, flawless in every sense, and in step with everything God asks; my ultimate question would be, "how could I ever cash in on redemption through faith?" I couldn't. The reason I could not cash out is because I would not need it from a behavioral standpoint, and nor would you. The truth is, we all fall short, not one of us are perfect, and the second we believe ourselves to be life has a way of humbling us. Know that our mistakes are the lowlights of our humanity, linking us to the highlights of God, the redeemer. That is where God can be most visibly – in our spirit and our flaws. Amidst our flawed nature, there is One who is always in agreement and perfecting our souls. Once we realize when we make mistakes and then subscribe to His ways above our own – we are acting in perfect faith.

❖ What mistakes have you held in your spirit that you have not let forgiveness and grace wash over?

❖ I am reminded constantly; once submitted to God, He promises that our transgressions are forgiven as far as east is from west. How does that scripture relate to question 1? Do you believe that new mercies are available for you every morning?

❖ Give 3 specific things that you have submitted to God where He redeemed those areas and allowed you to teach someone about the experience? If He hasn't yet, then what areas do you HOPE He redeems?

33.) Forgive and Forget for Yourself
(Luke 6:37)

Sometimes you screw the pooch in life, there is no way around it. By screwing the pooch, I mean make huge mistakes. Because of the mistakes I made through growth or immaturity, I sunk into a deep depression of guilt and shame, taking every second to look back into my past. I felt a loss of hope, as if I could not recover from the not so gracious fall I had taken. And because of this, I held onto memories, replayed moments in my mind to where if I could have had the conversation like this or ended things in this fashion maybe - it would have turned out different. After doing this and seeing others move on, I saw I was the only one still hanging on to dead friendships or dead events. I finally understood it was attached to forgiveness, and the one thing I had yet to do is forgive myself. I want to say this process will be an easy one, but I would be lying if I said that. It's one where you must understand what you did and choose not to walk in the way that you once did. It takes time and patience with yourself, pulling out the truth that the choices you made are the cause of where you are, but you are not condemned to stay there in your bad decisions. In this life we are going to make silly choices, get dirty, and make mistakes; it's inevitable. For example, if you were to fall in the mud and get dirt on your clothes; sensibly, you would get up, go home, and throw on a new outfit because you know walking around with dirty clothes makes no sense. And that is the essence of forgiveness of self; to know you fell and got dirty and you can change at any moment if you so choose.

❖ Why do you think forgiveness is important or not important?

❖ Jesus says forgive and you will be forgiven. This suggests that to get forgiveness we must be prepared to first give forgiveness, even to ourselves. How does that make you feel?

❖ Write down three things you have done that seem unforgivable and pray for a week that God opens your eyes to see how He has washed over those places with the blood. Record your findings.

34.) Run into the Eye of the Storm (Mark 4:35-41)

When the news forecast says there is a storm coming, we usually want to be nowhere close to it, moving as far away from it as possible. We find ourselves in the same position looking at the apostles all in a boat with Jesus, and suddenly a storm pops up. It is a lovely story in the book of Matthew if you are interested but I'll shorten it. The storm is happening, everyone is frightened and freaking out, but God is in ultimate control, the end. Sometimes, God will place a roadblock in our lives; an addiction, a person, an establishment, a disappointment or trial, and how ever long we prolong our due process is the length of time the season will last. We can be sure to lengthen the time waiting by not addressing the Elephant in the room to evolve. Yes, addressing it is going to hurt, it might embarrass you in a way that is humiliating, but you do not know what you could be if you confronted the worst parts of yourself. Who you truly are is not on the precipice of the storm but is found in the middle of all the chaos, ideas, and stories that you must navigate, in a boat, to arrive the shores of truth. Even still in that boat, God is with us through the storm. The same way God was with the apostles on their boat - Jesus was WITH them in the storm and had the power to calm the waves with the sound of His voice. But it teaches us something greater about the words we THINK we believe and when they actually are tested IN the storm. The eye of the storm, while daunting, can and will bring out the truest version of what you are, and what is in your heart. Instead of running away from the smoke, run to the eye of the storm with no fear and courage!

❖ What storm have you been avoiding the center of in your own life?

❖ The apostles were calmed after Jesus spoke to the storm. Do you believe that you can speak to your storm, and it has to cease because of the power of the name Jesus? Why or why not?

❖ What is the danger of not ever reaching the eye of the storm?

35.) Move Away from Energy Absorbers So You Can Claim Your Prize (Philippians 2:2)

Joel Osteen said, "If you spend too much time with the wrong people, you won't have time to dwell with the right people." While I do not agree with most of what Joel preaches and teaches – I do agree with this one statement. Who you are constantly around reflects yourself. A question I ask when I got to this point in life is – God, who are the right people? Through trial and error, He showed me those who energize your spirit and you charge them back up – people who uplift and encourage you to love boldly and take accounts for being wrong! The right people are also those you can help serve along the journey of life; thus, making it a mutually beneficial relationship. Mutual beneficial relationships are those that consist of both give and take; the people who you sow into and those who sow into you. Never allow for your energy to be zapped from you by people who have little or no life force. Ultimately, we are like energy outlets and people are plugs we allow into our walls. Yes, it's cool when the fan is running and the game is going, but when it's all said and done and they leave the house, it is you who must deal with the outrageous utility payment. Some people will ask you to foot the bill while you allow them to charge themselves from your blessings! As believers, we ought to be serving, but not at the expense of our self detriment. Be around those people who fill you up and you fill them, that way we can give more to those who need it.

❖ Do you have more people in your life who take energy from you or those who give to you?

❖ Think of the most giving person in your life, how do they inspire you to give more? How have you seen their giving impact the lives of others? Be very specific.

❖ Think of a friendship where you have given so much and what you were given was either squandered or not returned? How did that make you feel?

God says give without expecting anything in return; however, I think God wants us to be mindful that to give we must have something to give. In no way is this point moving away from that, it is more-so building awareness of when we're being taking from, we need to be aware so that we can fill up. Also, through how we live in Christ, we can choose to create a culture that is giving so we have more for kingdom purposes.

36.) Embrace Your Pain (James 1:2-4)

There is a lot to be said concerning how we can positively shape and alter our lives via social media platforms. We present our Sunday best and forget about the rest. Regardless of how peachy things may seem on the gram, behind the smiles and success, there is always pain, suffering, and heartache; and yet, we do not see those kinds of post very often... Even on my own journey to discovering who and what I was, I experienced pain to the utmost degree (and still do, but less impact than before.) In this time, I wanted success, but it alluded me, and why? I wasn't allowing God to make a miracle of my mess. I ignored my pain to survive because I felt if I stopped and embraced it surely, I would die – by feeling it all. Somewhere down the line, I convinced myself that showing my totality was something that made me weak, when in-fact my transparent weaknesses made me stronger because I knew I could face the judgement authentically. Showing my cuts, my scrapes, bruises, tenderness, and bumps is humility, but I could not accept it until I met myself in all those places, I was hiding from myself. When we accept the bad as an opportunity to redeem the good, we can virtually go through anything with amazing hope and self-assurance. When you embrace your pain, you will bleed out a little, it will hurt for a while, but you'll recover stronger than ever. The beauty is accepting what happened may have inflicted damage but not living IN or WITH the pain longer than necessary. The pain is a reminder to make strides to move onward in life with a different perspective.

❖ We all have those sore spots. Spots that if touched, it would send us into a spiral of pain because that hurt was left unaddressed and swept under the rug. What is a current pain in your life that you have been running from?

❖ How we deal with pain matters. If I asked you to examine how you dealt with the situation above, what is your response?

❖ Why would God choose not to heal our pain instantly? What is the reward of enduring or overcoming the obstacle that pain can bring to us?

37.) Heal
(Jeremiah 17:14)

Your mother just died… quick, I must do laundry, and I have fifty other tasks to accomplish today. You just lost all your friends, but before I feel something, I must run down this to-do list first. And we avoid it – put off our pain for a while; until it accumulates and burns – it burns from the inside out and at the most inconvenient time. Panic Attacks, depression, paralysis are some of the symptoms following the masking of our feelings. Look, I fully understand the responsibility of life, and it certainly does not stop because something happened to you personally, but I think a major issue in America is that we tend to keep moving because "too much is at stake." In turn, we medicate our issues and suppress them without addressing them or taking the time to heal properly. I am for prescription drugs, but what I am not for is not working through the issues of personal matters; a pill does not change you; you change you; weed does not change you, you change you. You must be okay with knowing that in this process of life you are going to get hit hard, and doing things with half a heart will produce half-hearted fruit, which will frustrate you even more! When life hits, we must take time to let the wound heal, or like an open wound, we risk infection and infections spread to create other problems in the body. If you desire to do anything great, you must heal, then move forward into recovery.

❖ What does "taking time to heal" imply and is that frustrating for you?

❖ How is healing vital for your purpose? Write down your main dream but also write the one thing you feel is holding you back from obtaining said dream. Now imagine your dream being brought to life by God only to carry that place of pain with you. How would that affect your vision? How would that effect the people who follow your steps in the vision God brought to life?

❖ Size up your biggest hurt in your life. Next, look up the definition of 'heal' and write it in the space below. Next, write (three times) 'I will heal from (Blank) no matter how long it takes.'

38.) Disrupt Your Patterns (Ephesians 4:22-24)

Have you ever been in a funk where you cannot seem to find your groove in life? Where it seems like life is passing you by while you are just watching from the backseat of the car and others are furiously (front seat) driving into their destiny and purpose. It's commonly known as a rut; or a pattern that we all happen to get stuck in. What does Webster's dictionary describe as a rut? A rut is a habit or behavior that has become dull, unproductive, but is very hard to change. So how do we get out of the rut? We must be diligent in changing our emotional states by disrupting behaviors that lead us into ruts. If you find yourself stuck in a ruttish pattern, expend all the energy you have in your soul to disrupt it by finding new ways to do that which you love. Maybe you have been running the same jogging route for five years now. What if you switched up your route & went another way? Maybe you have lived in the same town for a couple of years. Research where you'd like to be and take an intentional trip there to visualize what the future could look like if/when you decided to leave! Maybe you feel that squeeze where you have outgrown a certain friend group, and it is frightening to explore new options for a tribe; say goodbye in love and move on!

We must grow by being intentional about breaking our ruts and finding the gem in being uncomfortable; for that is when the true change will occur!

❖ What would you say is the biggest rut in your life that you feel stuck in?

❖ Oftentimes, the reason we won't change our patterns is because we fear what is on the other side of the unknown, and what is known is far more comfortable. What do you fear most about breaking the patterns that led you into the rut you currently dwell in? If you are not in a rut, write what you did to get out of it and what you learned from it?

❖ How is acknowledging a rut and taking steps to get out of it healthy for loving yourself?

39.) Understand Your Value and Worth (Psalm 139:14)

Value in sales is determined by the seller. The services rendered is only as valuable as the person or establishment believes it to be. Unlike products or services, we as a people cannot be sold, yet we do determine how we allow others to treat us depending on how we value ourselves. There came a time in my own personal/business life where I had to make a choice; either I was going to believe what others told me about my value and person, or I would believe what God told me about my value; not only as a gifted artist but also as a person. When you finally know and understand your value, you will begin to see things that do not reflect it and act accordingly by dismissing, changing, or evolving out of situations that do not add up. We mustn't feel bad about growth but view this transformation as part of the growing process that is confidence. Would Eric Thomas The Hip Hop Preacher sleep at a motel six? I mean he could, but overall, it does not reflect his personal or intrinsic values at his core. Would a Ferrari be caught dead at a CarMax (no disrespect to CarMax)? No, because Ferrari is so important, it has its own dealership for its own makes and models.

Yet that is exactly what we do when we entertain things that are lesser than everything we are called to be. What's crazy is that most people would object in their heads, "Well, who am I kidding, I'm no Ferrari, I'm more like a Honda Civic, the 1998 version..." And I am here to say that that is a lie from the enemy, and the truth is we are ALL sons and daughters, Kings and Queens of the Most High! Explore who God says you are and live in that value.

❖ Growing up, think back to comments made to you about your own value from parents, siblings, and friends alike… Did you hear positive affirmations or negative affirmations? Or did you not hear anything at all? Write down what memories you have about this below.

❖ Trailing behind the second question, how did hearing (or not hearing) about your value influence the way you feel about yourself now? What are some of the things you wish you had heard about who you are?

❖ I want to reestablish what God says about your value. Use a search engine online and look up "who God says I am" scriptures (or something to that effect) or scriptures about identity in Christ. Whenever we struggle with value it's only because we do not know who we are. In your findings, write down three scriptures below and let those three things be mantras for the next week when you forget who you are; allowing them to be seeds right now for the future of your value.

40.) Make an Effort to Be Confident (2<u>nd</u> Timothy 4:7)

There are plenty of people who struggle with confidence. We all fall short in the glory of God, but we especially fall short in our own eyes because of our unrealistic expectations of ourselves. Many of us want confidence in our lives, yet we find ourselves asking the question(s) "What is this thing confidence and how do I find it?" I want to let you in on the biggest secret—I was not always confident! It took an intentional effort to find my mojo of self-motivation to believe, even when I did not "feel" it or understand what it means to be confident. I learned how to fake it until I made it, and once I got it, I never lost that FEELING, and now you can have it too! Make a practice of being comfortable in all situations, and after faking it habitually, you will begin to generate an actual self-confidence that precedes the faking it took to get there. Even while explaining this theory to my friends, they always look at me and say I do not want to fake it, but before you make any dramatic life change you must to prime yourself to change. Also, before you are something, you have to attempt to be it. Eventually, the feeling that comes with "imposter syndrome" will pass and you'll break into who you are! When you know you are endorsed by the almighty father in heaven, you should walk with your chin up a little higher than the rest!

❖ In raising my daughter, I have learned about confidence. The more she feels loved and protected the more willing she is to risk and do more than she could ever think possible. When it comes to people who make you feel trusted, as if you can do anything, name the five closet people that fit the bill to that. What messages do they relay to you about being confident in yourself? If you do not have any, then your assignment is to work on finding one (or five) by the end of this month and building an intentional relationship.

❖ Why do you believe confidence has been a struggle to obtain for you personally?

❖ How does confidence relate to Corinthians 1-13? Do you believe that about yourself, and how should that change your own confidence?

41.) The Art of Silence (Isaiah 53:7)

Today, I woke up for quiet time to hear the wonderful preaching of my pastor Malcom Everest of Fireside Church. He spoke of the beauty of silence and how Jesus, while accused, belittled, and talked about never chose to respond to the allegations when Pharisees questioned who He was. I think we can learn something from Yeshua's example on how we ought to walk out confidence in our own lives. What we do is far more important than what we say, and everything that comes to us in the form of gossip, slander, or insults does not warrant a response from us. Jesus was focused on what His Father asked of Him – the work and His ultimate purpose. Who we are is the total of our actions that eventually expose the inner workings of our hearts. Our heart beats very softy, but without it, our whole body wouldn't be able to function. I believe God knows that we should be like our hearts; soft murmuring yet violently alive and working. In total, stick to what you do and move in silence instead of words. For six months, allow your actions lead everything you do and go on strike from speaking of plans - watch what happens! Everyone can doubt what you say, but very few can refute what you do.

❖ When thinking of being silent with success and advancements in life, how does that protect your overall vision you have for your life?

❖ Why do you think you have to defend yourself against slander, gossip or rumors?

❖ Where does the balance of silence fit in this social media age? Does the thought of not reporting your life story make you cringe, or does it feel like a relief? If God prompted you to give up reporting and instead learn for a year, would you be able to? Why or why not?

42.) Treat Yourself with Gentleness and Care (Proverbs 18:21)

We all know that we can easily become some of the harshest critics of ourselves, mainly because we lack confidence as people; however, we must wrestle with this so that we may come to a complete understanding of how to love ourselves. Most of the time, we weigh our actions on a scale in our head and if what we do does not match up to what our standard is, we consider it a loss. If we did not hit the target exactly - we must not be talented, we must not be great, we must not be children of the Most - High and that is so far from being true! We must expect to be imperfect and chose to direct our thoughts toward what reflects the truth of who we are, even when we do not FEEL ourselves and our low vibe behaviors at times. The best thing you can give when an individual is down is a kind sincere word from the heart, not harsh words and criticism. We easily consider this treatment for others but disregard the same for ourselves. So, I say, let us treat ourselves how we would like to be treated—with words of affirmation and a gentle steady heart. Not berating oneself when a mistake is made but understanding everything is a process.

Give yourself time to grow, time to heal, a time to change, and a time to understand. You'll love the results far more than you thought you would.

❖ How you talk about yourself really matters for maintaining the strength of the mind. If I pick your brain, what conversations do you have in your head about yourself? Whether positive or negative, write down the litany of thoughts you had after reading that question.

❖ After assessing your thoughts, what most do you feel needs to change about your thinking concerning yourself?

❖ Have you ever taken yourself out on a date? Should you be so bold – I suggest you try this. Sure, it will be awkward at first, but as you ease into this exercise, you'll see how long you have neglected yourself. Love your neighbor as you love YOURSELF. Take time to love you without guilt. Get dressed up – make a reservation but give it as a gift to you the way you might someone else. Record what you discovered below!

43.) Fix Your Mind to Focus on All That is GOOD (Philippians 4:8)

We all know—GOD is GOOD because God is LOVE. You'll often hear Christians say it to one another in passing, at a BBQ, a picnic, over the phone, but do we really mean it!? It's one thing to say it but it's another thing to focus your mind upon His goodness. When focused on the GOOD, we tend to see less bad, which in turn improves the quality of our lives. The view of goodness is only as truthful as the filter in which it passes through. Bad eyes, bad life, good eyes, blessed life. For example, yes, the car may have shut off on the freeway, but because of the GOODNESS of God, it didn't stop in the middle of traffic and have to be towed away. Because of GOODNESS you are safe, and while it may have broken down in the "bad side of town," God's angels kept you from harm's way. We always get stuck in the inconveniences of life and it is so easy to hold onto negative thoughts, but this shouldn't be so. God asks us to fix our eyes on heavenly things up above and to seek truth. It's a glorious thing when we can train our mind to move forward with joy THROUGH any obstacle, because that will be the foundation of our livelihood and faith to stand upon in a time of trouble. My encouragement? Get serious about seeing the good and fight for it every day.

❖ What is a situation today where something bad happened (or this week)? How long was it able to take up space in your thoughts? How did those thoughts affect your mental space?

❖ Think of that same situation above; where can you find the good in the problem; turning a negative perception into a positive perspective?

❖ The power of the mind can be very strong if used in the correct way. How does changing your thoughts about seeing the good in the problem effect how you feel overall about the situation? Are you able to do this with every problem that comes your way this week?

44.) Understand Your Season and Act Accordingly (Ecclesiastes 3:1)

There is nothing worse (and unbearable) than a person who is in the summer heat and is wearing winter clothes! You would give that person a crazy look and say, "Dude, WHAT are you wearing, my G!? You got on a coat and it's 5000 degrees outside!" That action, to normal eyes, would seem unreasonable; after all, we all know summertime is not the season to wear a winter coat, yet we do things like that in real life when we do not realize what season of life we are in. It would be obvious to say that this person's attire is out of season, and rightly so. God says that there is an anointed time and season for everything under the sun (Ecclesiastes 1) and naturally we must be able to have spiritual eyes to discern what time we are in. For instance, my wife and I have a seven-fold blessing that walks among us. We now understand (in maturity) if we just received a harvest then we know the next season we will have to sow something to receive another harvest for the next season. To maximize time, authority, and blessings, we must KNOW what season we are in by petitioning and meeting God in His established plans for our lives.

Be honest and take an assessment of what is going on around you in your life and adjust accordingly.

❖ What season of life do you feel you are in personally? A season of harvest? A season of bareness? A season of silence? A season of pain? In humility, is there anything that you have sown to contribute to the season you now stand in? Describe your season down below in full detail.

❖ Concerning seasons, the Bible talks about sowing (working/planting) seasons and harvest (receiving) seasons; concerning the current season in your life, what season are you in? How are you certain you are in that season (what fruit is showing)?

❖ How can actions being "out" of season affect you and others around you? Are there any behaviors, places, ideas you feel might not be best for this season in your life?

45.) Look in the Mirror and Tell Yourself That You Love You (Mark 12:31)

Culture does a fantastic job of making sure that we tell others we love each other almost every second of our day, but we never say it (I love you) to the person in the mirror. I asked myself on my journey, "WHY?" This is so important and healthy for people, yet no one ever considers the impact that it can truly have. We are so quick to tell others we love them; we will go down the list of why's; I love you because… The reason why I love you so much is… The one thing the world convinced us of is that it is selfish to LOVE ourselves. It is funny because our FATHER says that you can only LOVE others as MUCH as you LOVE YOURSELF. I wouldn't say we ought to, or it might be nice to love ourselves but that we NEED to love ourselves! We should speak powerful affirmations to ourselves, we need to declare that we are children of the most high God and that we are successful because we are walking in His marvelous calling for our lives. We need to always be ready to look in the mirror and affirm the love that we have for ourselves, even on the days we look a mess, or we haven't quite hit the mark and fall flat on our faces. So, what you fell?! - You are STILL worthy of love despite all blunders and mistakes.

❖ QUICK! It cannot wait! Find a mirror, look yourself in the eye, and tell you that you love who you are. If you are not by a mirror, then pick up a phone and record a video of you saying you love you and why you love you (At least 3 reasons)! (Thought you could get out of it, huh? I know you got your smart phone on you!)

❖ For seven days, I want you to say you love yourself in the mirror AND give yourself three positive affirmations; recording what it made you feel like each day and write all the affirmations down here. When you are done with the week, look at all the reasons you love yourself. Also, the reasons cannot be the same, meaning each day you must find a new awesome thing you love about you!

❖ How can you love yourself more each day?

46.) Stop Lying… To You or Anyone Else (Colossians 3:9)

Did you know it is clinically proven that when one lies it causes internal stress upon your body? This is exactly how polygraphs are used, they are connected to detection, not of the lie itself but the amount of stress that the participant displays while hooked up to the machine. So, what does this say about our very essence as human beings as well as kingdom subjects? Lying causes stress and therefore if we want to live a peaceful life, as we were called, then we had better stop lying and just be honest at all cost. Challenge yourself in this but speak nothing but truths over your life and the lives of others, biblical truths. Whenever someone asks you a question, do not jump around the field, tap-dancing a reply, be straightforward and honest with a gentle answer. I want us to all find ways that we can replace our timid responses into full-fledged truthful statements. At times we can be tricked to believe the truth may be harmful to the listener; however, once we lie, we place the stress upon ourselves, and it's hard to walk in peace with stress in our hearts. Avoid that altogether and whenever approached with conflict or a concern try your best to be honest. People might not always like what you have to say; however, people will always follow you if they can trust you at your word. Stop lying to you about who you are and stop lying to others, it does nothing for anyone!

❖ Why do we/you believe that even little lies are permissible? What are excuses that you make to tell someone a lie and you know the truth?

❖ How has lying hurt you in the past? What did that make you feel like when someone told you a lie straight up to your face and you knew it?

❖ If you had an external motivation to stop lying altogether, what would it be?

47.) Attack the Day (Ephesians 5:16)

In war, there are two people on the battlefield: the winners and the losers. In war, we fight. In war, we strategize. In war, we plan and then we execute. The best way to loving yourself is to create a beautiful blueprint for your life; however, most people get bogged down in the details and figuring out the why's of life; which is important but not everything. One thing we must understand is we can figure out the why of life, but without substance, character, and a hard work ethic, we will not be able to sustain them, and that is where attacking the day comes in. Sometimes (and trust me, I know, I can be so passive about my own days) we think passively, stating things such as "I'll get something done later" or "I will attempt that dream in ten years" or "I will when I am ready," while tomorrow is not promised. I wear a watch that reads 0:00 to remind me I do not have time to waste and today could be my last day, so I might as well go at it with a BANG! Ultimately, if you have a thought or an idea; simply do it. If you think about your plan of action, then you might as well take a step toward it and attack it. Until you wake up and plan to fight for it, you cannot be a winner on the battlefield of life. Keep pushing and attacking it with all that you have within you!

❖ What is a thought in your head that keeps you from attacking the day?

❖ How can you better plan your attacks, with your own weaknesses in mind? (For example, I am terrible at tracking progress so what helps me is when at the end of the week, I write down all that I have done.)

❖ How can you better plan your attack on the day so your execution can be better? List three ways.

48.) Never Touch Anything with Half Your Heart (Colossians 3:23)

Full is such a great word. In my own words, to be filled is to be inflated with substance, ready to be released or poured out onto anyone or anything. The concept of us as humans being full of love is a beautiful phenomenon. The reason why being full is so important for us as believers is fullness helps you understand what makes you come to life—the gift that you have inside of you that will help shape the world for the better. So, I would like for you to ask yourself a question: "What FULLY makes you come alive and is connected to your HIGHER purpose." What sparks your heart to life is what makes you full "for where your treasure is, there your heart will also be." There is no way that any of us can imagine reaching our fullest potential by touching any endeavors with half our heart. Would you try to play regulation pool with half a stick? Have a sparring match with half a sword? What about being given a test and turn it in halfway through? You see where I am going here? When we halfheartedly pursue something, it shows a poor follow through in the results; you get a mixed bag. When God promises a thing; He delivers, and that is why we can TRUST Him to do what He says He'll do. If we are to walk in the fullness of loving who we are created to be; whenever we do anything; "meaningless" jobs, performance opportunities, loving on our neighbor, we ought to go at it with 100% as if reflecting the glory of God through every fiber of our being. Let us make an agreement to never touch anything with half our hearts again.

❖ Reflect for one moment, can you think of a time where you have been asked to do something and fulfilled that obligation with a level of half-heartedness? What was the result?

❖ What are three ways to avoid doing things with half-heartedness?

❖ Who is someone who does something with 100% effort in your life? What is usually their result and how can you model that as inspiration in your life to grow? If you do not have anyone in your immediate life, maybe it may be an artist – educator or teacher.

49.) Set Some Boundaries; Be Okay with Standards (Proverbs 4:26)

Imagine a garden. In this garden you see plush flowers everywhere; beautiful bountiful colors, an anointing of strength and healthiness among the plants, row upon row of roses, peonies, and sunflowers; lined up perfectly sitting; waiting to be seen. As far as the eye can see these plants are special, suggesting an intentional touch of excellence through their cultivation. As your eyes stream across the garden you notice right in the middle there is a circle of dead plants; smelly, bug eaten, rotten, unkept flowers. As far as you can see, you would also know that those flowers are out of place in the garden. It is easily recognized in a metaphorical garden, but do we view our lives in that same fashion? If you catch nothing else, understand that boundaries help preserve your standard in your life's garden. It promotes order. Simply put, dead flowers do not belong with living flowers. If your life is the garden, then you have to realize when we set high standards for ourselves and others around us, it will cultivate a beautiful, streaming, consistent, healthy way of life that is pleasing, not only unto others watching but also to our Father. When we allow organizations and people to dismiss firm boundaries put in place, we set ourselves up for an inconsistent life; flourishing in some ways, dead in other spaces, when we have the capacity to be beautiful all around! And who knows, by your quality of living, you may turn someone onto the way of following God and grooming their garden as a result. Set a standard in your life, do not allow just anyone to plant anything, at any time, and you will begin to see love and enjoy your own unique garden.

❖ Upon reading this prompt, what were the first three issues that came to mind that might slow your garden (of life) from flourishing in all its splendor?

❖ How have those things or those people held you up in loving yourself? If yes, in what particular ways?

❖ To love ourselves, we must measure our life with specificity, or we will accept everything that everyone else defines as love toward ourselves. Set some standards for your life in specific places. I want you to consider friends, family, and workplace. Set three standards (for each) in which you will set and expect others to hold up their end in respect for your personal growth. Now, in holding them to a standard you must also adhere to them on your end as well. Writing these out will help gain a proper perspective of what is needed from you but also what you can expect to see in the next chapter of your life.

50.) Let Yourself Soar (Proverbs 29:18)

There comes a time when you hit the corner in your destiny. Be it a career path or a mental makeover, you'll always have to let go of something or someone to grab hold of the next thing that God has prepared for you in life. It is going to hurt, there is no easy way around it; it is going to feel bad; moments of doubt may arise, and this change may prompt feelings of resentment, anger, or ill will. One thing I learned in my late twenties that I would like to pass on is that you have got to allow yourself to soar. A bird cannot fly with weight on its wings; it will remain grounded if it does not find way to shake off the excess and fly. What I mean by that is when you allow yourself to soar, you can establish the path that God has put you on. You must remember; soaring is not just about you; it's about the others who need you to fly so that they can be inspired by your taking off. Everyone is inspired by the one who made it because it forces them to examine what they are currently doing in their life and ask, "Well, am I going to fly like them or am I going to stay **here** all my life?" Maybe you are being promoted out of a season of life where you simply cannot continue in certain relationships, jobs, or surroundings.

The best thing you can do for yourself and the people who are looking at you for leadership and inspiration is to go ahead and let people go and allow yourself to soar. Your journey is just beginning – you never have to chase what its yours. Infact your new mantra should be "I do not chase, I attract."

❖ Why do you think that letting go is hard for you? What should you let go of in this moment that is too heavy to keep carrying?

❖ What are the weights that hold you down? Many things can keep one grounded; negative thoughts about self, other people's negative opinions of you, the pressure of life. Identify your own weights and trust your inner voice.

❖ Sometimes people have a fear of flying because it's too high and ascends them to altitudes of which they have never been before. Do you have a fear of becoming everything you were meant to be? How do you sabotage that when you have gotten closer to your soaring moment?

51.) Allow Yourself to Start a New Chapter (Isaiah 43:19)

There is a time when you have become so accustomed to doing things one way your whole life it almost becomes second nature. It may be a passion, a job occupation, a dream, but in that conformability, it almost becomes stagnant, and you could perform the task or do the job with your eyes closed. As you continue, you keep, asking yourself, "Is there more to me and my life and what I have to offer, or will I continue on in the same way, doing the same thing, living the same life year after year." NO! The Lord says to His people, *"Behold, I am doing a NEW thing. Can YOU not perceive it?"* Understand when you grab ahold of the NEW, the OLD must be let go of. Sometimes, God will bring you to a certain place in life for you to learn about a specific period but then promote you to a new, higher level - accept it. The best thing you can do for your life and your faith is to allow yourself to be free and start to believe/walk in the newness of your call. You may be nervous, you may not see all the steps but just know that we walk not by sight but by faith. Start your new journey today.

❖ What has become old or stagnant in your walking life? How does it make you feel on the inside?

❖ What is something new that you are uncertain of but gives you so much joy and happiness? What are key events that make you say, I could see myself doing this?

❖ It is possible to get anywhere you desire. If you see it in your mind, you can have it in your walking life. You just must make choices that reflect your desire so that you move toward that goal. Write down everything you see for yourself in the future and become it or move toward it every day for the rest of your life. Become what you want most, and that is how you love yourself from the inside out.

52.) BONUS Xpress Yourself Daily

In 2015, in the heartbeat of Houston, Texas, I began what would become the foundation of my life's work—**Xpression Pedagogy**. Rooted in hip hop culture but open to the rhythm of all creative voices, this practice was born from the need for a safe space where interdisciplinary artists—dancers, poets, musicians, painters, and storytellers alike—could gather not to impress, but to *Xpress*. It wasn't about perfecting a step, hitting a high note, or finishing a piece or winning a battle. It was about showing up with your full emotional truth. Whether it was joy, rage, sorrow, or curiosity, **Xpression Pedagogy** invited everyone to move, speak, and create from that raw, honest place. I've seen how powerful this can be—how someone's truth, shared in movement or verse, can spark healing in another. But I've also seen what happens when people grow older and slowly lose that outlet. Somewhere along the way—between jobs, expectations, responsibilities, and the fear of judgment—a lot of us tuck our expressions away. We don't mean to. Life just starts demanding more silence from the parts of us that once shouted freely. And so many grown folks I meet are walking around like closed books—feelings locked behind tired eyes, creativity gathering dust.

But here's the truth: the need to express doesn't vanish with age. It waits. Sometimes it whispers in our anxieties, in our stiffness, in our restless nights. Other times it screams in our arguments, our shutdowns, our deep disconnection. Xpression is not a luxury. It's a necessity. And when we suppress it, it shows up in ways we don't expect. So let me offer this to you—not as a fix-all, but as a re-opening:

Ways to Reclaim Your Xpression

1. Move without purpose

Set aside five minutes a day to move in your space. No structure, no music if you don't want it. Let your body speak what your mouth won't. Shake. Rock. Slam your feet. Flow soft. Just move *with* your feeling, not around it.

2. Talk to yourself with respect

Say out loud what you're feeling. Not what you *should* feel. Not what you think sounds wise. Just say it: "I'm angry." "I feel numb." "I miss being free." Speak it to a mirror, a journal, a voice note. Let your truth be heard—by you. Name the emotion out loud so its not held in!

3. Find your cipher and transmute it:

Surroundyourselfwithatleastoneortwopeoplewhoare committed to truth-telling, Xpression, and emotional honesty. Build a space—digital or in-person—where the main rule is: *No judgment. Only Xpression. Dance, music, beat-making, monologues, CREATE*

4. Create just to feel, not to finish

Draw. Sing. Write. Dance. Don't worry about making it "good." Just make. Let the act of creating be your release. Your offering. Your therapy.

❖ When did you first learn it wasn't safe or acceptable to express how you truly feel?

❖ What would my day look like if I led with my honest emotion instead of my expectations?

❖ How can I help someone else unlock their expression by unlocking my own?

*Remember - you don't have to be perfect. You must be present with your truth. And the moment you choose to Xpress love to yourself again, you reconnect with a version of you that never stopped creating—only got quiet for a while.
Welcome back, and I cannot wait to see who you'll become after this*

Acknowledgements

I thank God OUR Father, who gave me the trials up to this point and the courage to overcome them to help change and influence the way people think around the world. I prayed and I prayed that He might use me in a way that is pleasing to Him yet be unconventionally myself. I have been in hiding for too long in fear of what others might think of how I am or if I am "Christian" enough, yet I found I was most effective when I was acting in my purest form, just existing, not worried about "their" rules. I lived in shame for so long and I feel like this is my breakout moment to express myself in a totally new way. In trusting myself, I found that God's voice in my life trumps! I do not have fear of being myself and sharing my story and I know this is just the beginning. Thank you to my wife Maddy Rochelle for trusting that the only way this vision could come to life was through our move to Greenville SC. It sounds crazy, because we moved from what seemed like a major market; Houston in a house, and "downsized" in opportunity to trade for what God wanted to do with our lives. She is the ONLY reason I have been able to see the real person I am and trust that what I have inside of me is beautiful in all forms and in all ways. Thank you for always believing in me, even when you didn't have a ledge to step out on in the crazy vision God gave me in my head through dreams.

You were with me when we were on food stamps to being the woman beside me when this book became a bestseller. I love you and I thank God—it could only have been you in this life journey with me. To my loving sweet daughter Addelynn Grace Rochelle; Peach, I love you. By the time this book is published, you will be seven going on eight (prophetically speaking), and Papa wants to tell you that I would have never ever attempted to do things of this caliber if I didn't understand that the legacy of our future didn't depend on it. Every morning, I wake up, I move toward you and see the beauty that you bring to both me and mama's life, and I promise you that because of that I will never quit, I will not rest, and I will not stop until you can rest securely in the dream and vision that papa has for our family. I love you dearly and thank you so much for being you! This is a brand spanking new edition as this book took almost 8 years to create but since the conception; my wife has given birth to our son Jaelynn Howard Rochelle a.k.a Pickle and let's just say inspiration shot through the roof after having my lil fella! Homie -you inspire me to go hard because now I have a road dog for life! Love you and we are going to stay closer than a clam in its shell. Also - shout out to Phoebe Marie-Lynn Rochelle due late August! To Mama (Mimi) and Dad (Pop-pop,) thank you for always helping our family and being aids to what we thought we could do and what we thought we couldn't do. You have been more than supports – counselors – loan officers – wise counsel – best friends and so much more! To Grammy, Grand Po-Po and GiGi thank you so much for sticking by us through thick and thin and being there for our children with such passion and devotion! To Tia and my loveliest nieces and best cousins– best playmates ever and we'd do anything for you! Lastly to every mentor, professor, teacher, cipher or dancefloor - to my enemies, those who never liked me and never will, thank you so much sincerely. Your love or hate really helped set me free. You taught me things about myself that helped me transmute my pain into purpose for others. AGH – I FREAKIN love you all so much and weather good or bad influence – you helped me accomplish this feat and without being bitter. I want YOU to prosper as your soul prospers, but I firmly believe you can only do that when you love yourself. Thank you to everyone who supported TEAM ROCHELLE and helping us gather the beauty of our own ashes, allowing Christ to use them as inspiration, transforming them into life for you to change and be all that you can be.